WHERE LEGENDS LIVE

A PICTORIAL GUIDE TO CHEROKEE MYTHIC PLACES

BY DOUGLAS A. ROSSMAN

ILLUSTRATED BY NANCY-LOU PATTERSON

PHOTOGRAPHS BY
WILLIAM E. SANDERSON & DOUGLAS A. ROSSMAN

PUBLISHED BY
CHEROKEE PUBLICATIONS
CHEROKEE, NORTH CAROLINA

Published by

CHEROKEE   PUBLICATIONS

P. O. Box 256

Cherokee, NC 28719

Publishers and distributors of American Indian Books

(send for free catalog)

1st Printing . . . January 1988 . . . 15,000

ISBN #0-935741-10-0

CONTENTS

DEDICATION

This book is dedicated to the Cherokee people, with admiration and respect.

ACKNOWLEDGMENTS

In the course of a project such as this, one incurs debts, both large and small, to numerous generous people. My sincere thanks go to: Carol and Robert Brown, Conyers, Georgia, for encouragement from "the beginning" and for making their home a cheery way station along the route of the quest; Richard Bruce, Western Carolina University, Cullowhee, North Carolina, for suggesting the best vantage points for photographing Cheoah and Whiteside mountains; Robert Bushyhead, Cherokee, North Carolina, for helping to locate a number of sites near Cherokee and for his patience, good humor, and linguistic prowess while converting the names given by Mooney (1900) into his own phonetic system; Bill Cook, Johnson City, Tennessee, for consulting with Bushyhead on the final draft of the linguistic material; George Ellison, Bryson City, North Carolina, for sharing his knowledge of the Nantahala Gorge; Sam Gray, Western Carolina University, for a copy of his attractive exhibition book, *Mythic Maps;* Lena Martin, Murphy, North Carolina, for finding out the exact location of "Leech place"; Joyce Nelson, Louisiana State University, for her patience with my many requests for the loan of yet another topographic map; Nancy-Lou Patterson, University of Waterloo, Ontario, for devoting so much of her time and talent to the creation of the beautiful illustrations for this book; Dan Pitillo, Western Carolina University, for the loan of his slides of Big Bald Mt., Gregory Bald, and Stratton Bald, from which the pictures for this book were made; Nita Rossman, for typing the manuscript, for accompanying me on the first trip, and for tolerating the diversion of her husband's time and family resources to this project; Bill Sanderson, Montreat, North Carolina, for his photographic expertise and, especially, for his companionship; John Saye, Tallulah Falls, Georgia, for generously granting permission to reprint a photograph of one of the falls from his book, *The Life and Times of Tallulah . . . The Falls, The Gorge, The Town;* Judith Schiebout, Louisiana State University, for her moral support of the project; Kay and Ed Sharpe, Cherokee, North Carolina, for their interest and encouragement, but most of all for inviting two strangers into their home and making them feel like "family"; and Tom Underwood, Cherokee, North Carolina, for help in locating several sites near Cherokee and for numerous other courtesies, especially in letting us use his shop (Medicine Man Crafts) as a headquarters when we were in the area. I would also like to take this opportunity to express my appreciation to two old friends who, though not directly involved with this project, nevertheless had an influence on its creation: Kelly Smith, Fairfield, Illinois, my dormmate at Southern Illinois University, who helped to focus my intense, but diffuse, interest in the American Indian on his people, the Cherokee; and Alyce Johnston, Chunchula, Alabama, who introduced me to the Cherokee language during the several years we team taught an informal "Cherokee Language and Culture" course at Louisiana State University.

PRONUNCIATION GUIDE

Cherokee was not a written language until the early 1800's when the brilliant mind of Sequoyah devised an alphabet of 85 letters to accomodate the sounds of spoken Cherokee. This system is, of course, unintelligible to readers of English, for whom Cherokee names have inevitably been rendered phonetically. Over the years a number of different phonetic systems have been used (some without explanation), but no standard usage has been established. In this book, in addition to using the more or less traditional spellings, I have been fortunate to have the generous cooperation of Cherokee linguist Robert Bushyhead, who has converted the names given by Mooney (1900) into the phonetic system devised by Bushyhead and Cook (unpublished *MS*). Bushyhead also has verified or modified the translations given by Mooney, and has provided translations for names that Mooney did not. Where Bushyhead's pronunciations -- which have been italicized -- differ slightly from those of Mooney, it may be because of dialectic differences; Bushyhead is a Kitu-hwa speaker and some of Mooney's words appear to have been rendered in the Overhill dialect. For instance, *yo:na* versus *yo:nv* for bear.

The following guide to pronunciation is adapted from the Bushyhead and Cook manuscript. Cherokee has six, rather than five, vowel sounds: *a, e, i, o, u,* and *v.* The *a,* sounds like the "a" in father, the *e* like the "a" in date, the *i* like the "ee" in feet, the *o* like the "aw" in saw, the *u* like the "u" in flute, and the *v* like the "u" in uncle. These vowels may be of short duration (and are unmarked) or they may be held (and are followed by a :). Accented vowels are pronounced with a slightly higher pitch than are unaccented vowels (and bear an accent mark ').

The letters *y, w, l, n,* and *m* are resonants and are pronounced the same way they are in English except when preceded by an *h,* which indicates that the resonant sounds are whispered. For example, *y* sounds like the "y" in you, *hy* like the beginning of hew; *w* sounds like the "w" in witch, *hw* like the "wh" in which. The other resonants are similarly modified, but there are no corresponding whispered sounds in English.

The letters *k* and *t* are pronounced like the English "g" and "d," respectively, except when followed by an *h.* Then they sound like the English "k" and "t," respectively, but with the "h" also pronounced. The letter *s* is pronounced as if it were followed by an "h" as in the English she; the letter *h* sounds like the "h" in he.

The combination *ts* sounds like the English "j" or "dz," depending on the speaker.

A brief pause made in the back of the throat, as indicated by the hyphen in the English negative huh-uh, is called a glottal stop and is indicated by the symbol ˀ.

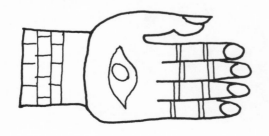
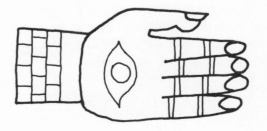

INTRODUCTION

In 1900 the famous American ethnologist James Mooney published his now classic *Myths Of The Cherokee*. Although a few stories that he had not collected have since appeared in print, most notably in Kilpatrick and Kilpatrick (1966), Mooney's book remains the most comprehensive collection of Eastern Cherokee myths and legends ever compiled. Many of the stories have a vague mythic setting, but a large number are associated with specific features of the southern Appalachian landscape,* and Mooney described their locations with a fair degree of prescision although he provided a picture only of Nikwasi Mound. In order to visualize more clearly the other mythic sites, it became my personal quest to visit and photograph as many of them as I could find. It soon occurred to me that other people in the region, both residents and visitors, might enjoy learning about the significance of these places, and thus the idea for this book was born. Subsequently, William E. Sanderson became the project's principal photographer and soon made the quest his own, too. Like all true quests, ours had internal as well as external dimensions, and the places we experienced and the people we met in our search for the mythic sites contributed to our spiritual growth. Despite the disappearance of many sites beneath TVA lakes and the alteration of some by still other manifestations of "progress," some of the places we visited still possess the ability to arouse in a receptive visitor the sense of being in the presence of something extraordinary. It seems almost inevitable that such places would have myths connected with them.

Why make such a fuss over myths and mythic place, one might ask. Isn't a myth something that is untrue and, therefore, has no value other than as mere entertainment? It is, indeed, unfortunate that in Western culture's swing toward ultrarationalism we have dismissed or forgotten the chief meaning of myth and have settled for a secondary, and actually contradictory, definition of the term. Myths are a symbolic expression of Man's understanding of his relationship to the Universe and, as such, provide each culture with a map of Man's spiritual landscape. The interested reader is urged to pursue the subject in Joseph Campbell's highly informative and readable *Myths To Live By* (1973).

———

* Cherokee mythology is not unique in being associated with specific geographic features. That situation has characterized most, if not all, mythic systems. If it seems strange to many European-Americans, that probably reflects how far removed they have become--both temporally and spatially--from their own mythological roots.

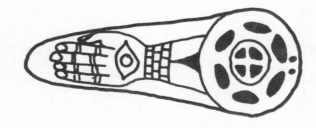

CHEROKEE MYTHOLOGY
(A LEGENDARY BACKGROUND)

The Cherokee mythic world view is generally similar to that of the other Southeastern Indian tribes and has been discussed in detail by Hudson (1976). Because Mooney's *Myths Of The Cherokee* is still readily available, I have not attempted to retell any of the stories in its entirety. What I have tried to do in the following paragraphs is to provide enough background that the reader can appreciate the significance of each mythic site from the brief comments accompanying each photograph. For ease in reading I have anglicized the Cherokee names of the various mythical beings, but the first time a name appears a phonetic spelling of the Cherokee name is also given. These names also appear in the index on p. 46.

In Cherokee mythology, many animals that normally live on the surface of the land are--in certain special places--believed to live underground or underwater. Rabbits (site 27) and bears (10, 16, 27) usually are associated with subterranean council houses. Underwater animals include bison (28, 57), "red dogs" (14), and bears (41). In other special places, giant individuals of animals normally to be expected in that habitat can be found: hornets (23), yellowjackets (3, 5), fishes (6, 44), lizards (24, 32), turtles (20), frogs (40), snakes (19, 39), and leeches (25).

The Nuhnehi

An entirely different group of beings who are frequently associated with underground or underwater dwellings (sites 7, 13, 17, 18, 30, 46, 49, 52) are the Nuhnehi *(Nv:ne'hi,* "Those who have always been here"). Although usually invisible, when they can be seen the Nuhnehi are like the Cherokee in appearance. The Nuhnehi are friendly toward them and have, on more than one occasion, even fought on behalf of the Cherokee when the latter were in danger of being overwhelmed by their enemies.

The Thunders

The Thunders (or Thunderers) are the most powerful spirit folk and they, too, are usually favorably disposed toward the Cherokee because of assistance once given Kanati *(Khana':ti),* Thunder, during his life-and-death struggle with a giant horned serpent. Kanati, his wife Selu *(Se:lu,* the corn spirit), and their two sons (the Thunder Boys) once lived atop Pilot Mountain (site 30) in what is now Transylvania Co., North Carolina, but following Selu's death Kanati and his sons seem to have moved westward, for we find them to be the focus of a major myth located in the rugged Tennessee River gorge a short distance downstream from present-day Chattanooga. Another of Kanati's sons, Lightning, who was borne by a human mother, had his body covered with sores. The boy sought out his father to be cured of his affliction. Kanati put him into a pot of boiling water and had his wife cast the pot, boy and all, into the Tennessee River (p. 34). Lightning emerged from the river with a whole skin, but the pot remained to form a large eddy where the water swirled above it (site 33).

After becoming acquainted with his half-brothers, the Thunder Boys, Lightning challenged the wily gambler Uhtsayi *(V:tsayi')* to play the disc-and-spear game that Uhtsayi had invented (and which, known as "chunkey," was popular among all Southeastern Indians). In a series of contests Uhtsayi wagered and lost everything he owned. In desperation he wagered his own life--and lost again. Trying to flee his fate, Uhtsayi changed his shape several times, each time being revealed when the Thunder Boys' pet beetle struck the gambler on the forehead, which gave off a metallic ring. Finally Uhtsayi was captured, tied with a grapevine, and staked to the bottom of the river (p. 34). There he is to remain until the end of the world, much like his Norse trickster counterpart, Loki. One cannot help but wonder if his periodic struggles to free himself are thought to be the cause of earthquakes, as was said to be the case with Loki.

The Nuhnehi and the Thunders have recently been discussed by Fogelson (1982) along with several kinds of dimunitive relatives collectively referred to as the Yuhwi Tsunsdi *(Yv:wi tsu:nsti),* the Little People (sites 3, 23). The relationship of the latter to the Cherokee has been more ambiguous than that of the larger spirit folk, who are almost always kindly. The Little People can be very helpful (returning lost objects or strayed children), but they can also throw rocks and play mean tricks on individuals to whom they have taken a dislike. There is even one legend in which Little People killed a Cherokee warrior (site 23).

Spearfinger
by Nancy-Lou Patterson

8

Spearfinger

One of the most feared mythical monsters in Cherokee country was Utluhtu *(U:thlvhtu)* or, as she was known in English, Spearfinger. Although she was an accomplished shapechanger, her true form was that of an old woman (cover; p. 8). That doesn't sound so fearful, one might think, but Utluhtu had a long bony forefinger on her right hand with which she would stab and extract the liver from her unsuspecting victim, often a child who only saw in her a kindly old grandmother. Frequently the victim was unaware his liver had been stolen until be began to weaken for no apparent reason, and by then it was just a matter of time until he died.

Spearfinger wandered far and wide through Cherokee country, but her favorite haunts seemed to be the Nantahala Gorge (site 19) and near the Little Tennessee River where it passes around the foot of Chilowee Mountain (site 55). On one occasion, to make her travels easier, she started to build a bridge of rocks up through the sky from Tree Rock on the Hiwassee River (site 48) to Whiteside Mountain. She had the job well underway when lightning shattered the bridge, breaking off its foundation on the western end of Whiteside Mountain (site 21) and scattering rocks along the ridge east of Tree Rock. Apparently the Thunders had taken offense at Spearfinger's bridge, or her behavior in general, or both.

Because Spearfinger could take on the appearance of anyone, the Cherokee came to fear and distrust not only strangers, but their friends and neighbors as well. This situation soon became intolerable, so the people held a council and decided to try to lure Utluhtu into a trap. They dug a deep pit in a woodland trail and, after concealing the opening with brush, they built a fire nearby to attract Spearfinger. They hoped she would think the fire had been made by a hunting party and would come in search of a lone hunter whose liver she could steal.

The plan worked beautifully, but when the warriors began to shoot at the monster trapped in the pit they discovered to their dismay that Spearfinger's skin was as hard as rock so that their arrows shattered when they struck her. A titmouse, perched overhead and watching the proceedings, began to sing a note that sounded to the Cherokee like the word "heart." Accordingly, they aimed at where they thought Spearfinger's heart should be and launched another flight of arrows. Alas, these, too, were broken. Enraged by what they perceived as a lie

on the part of the titmouse, the warriors cut off its tongue and to this day all titmice have had a short tongue.

Then another little bird, the chickadee, flew down into the pit and landed on Spearfinger's right hand. The warriors took this behavior to mean that they should shoot at that spot, which they proceeded to do, and soon one of their arrows pierced her wrist at the point where the spearlike finger joined it. Utluhtu died on the spot, and the chickadee has been known as a truthteller and bearer of good news ever since.

The Uktena

Another dreaded monster in the Cherokee mythic world is the Uktena *(U:khthe:nv)*, a giant serpent so dangerous that even to look upon one could be fatal (sites 5, 11, 12, 35, 36, 37). The Uktena is said to have a body that is as thick as a tree trunk and covered with glittering scales; on its head are a pair of horns (antlers?) and a huge shining crystal, the Uluhsati *(U:lvhsaʔti)*. The Uluhsati is greatly prized because to possess one insures its owner success in hunting, love, rainmaking, and every other activity, but especially in being able to foretell whether someone will live or die. Unfortunately the bright light from the crystal will befuddle a man's senses so that he would run toward the Uktena and thus become its victim.

Only one man is known to have succeeded in killing an Uktena and securing the magic crystal. He was a war captive of the Cherokee, a great Shawnee conjuror named Oganunitsi *(O:kanu:ni:tsi,* "Groundhogs' Mother").* The Cherokee were going to kill him, but they released him when he pledged to seek out and secure the Uluhsati. He searched the entire length of the Great Smokies and beyond, encountering a series of giant reptiles, amphibians, and fishes along the way (sites 9, 25, 32, 40), but it wasn't until he reached Cohutta Mountain (12) in what is now north-central Georgia that he finally found the Uktena he had been seeking. Oganunitsi built a

---

* "Groundhogs' Mother" seems to be a most unusual name for a man. I would like to suggest the possibility that he had found and cared for some newly orphaned baby groundhogs, and that they then followed him about as they would have their own mother. Someone observed this and jestingly gave him the name that stuck.

circular trench on the mountainside, set fire to the pine cones encircling the trench, and then shot an arrow into the seventh spot on the body pattern of the Uktena, which had been sleeping on the mountaintop. He evaded the rush of the mortally wounded serpent and leaping beyond the fire and trench was protected from the stream of venom spewed out by the Uktena in its death throes (p. 12). After seven days had passed the birds of the forest had stripped the carcass so completely that only the Uluhsati remained. Oganunitsi carried the magic crystal back to the Cherokee (site 4), who were said by Mooney to still have it in their possession as recently as 1890.

Hudson (1978) presented a lengthy discussion in which he saw a marked similarity between the Uktena and the dragon of Chinese mythology.

The Tlanuwa

Cherokee bird mythology is dominated by the figure of the Tlanuwa *(Thla'nu':wa)*, the great mythic hawk said to be capable of carrying off a man, a deer, or a bear. Although Mooney tentatively identified the goshawk as the bird known to the Cherokee as the "little tlanuwa," and Witthoft (1946) thought that it might be the broad-winged hawk, Howard (1968) argued on behavioral grounds that the "little tlanuwa" probably is the peregrine falcon. The latter interpretation was accepted by Hudson (1976) and is further supported by the alleged nest sites of the great Tlanuwa, both of which are on sheer cliff faces along rivers (sites 26, 38). The pair that nested on the cliff on the north side of the Little Tennessee River opposite the mouth of Citico Creek (site 26) had a tendency to carry off dogs and young children from the Cherokee villages. Finally a conjuror lowered himself down by a rope and pushed the four baby Tlanuwas into the river where they were swallowed up by an Uktena, the giant horned serpent (p. 47). The parent birds attacked the Uktena, tore it to pieces, and dropped the pieces onto the river bank where they made holes in the rock from the force of their impact (site 48).

Tsulkala

The other major mythical being who is associated with specific locations is Tsulkala *(Tsu:hlkala)*, the slant-eyed giant who owns all the game animals in the mountains. Although his height is never specified, others of his kind are said to be twice as tall as a man. Tsulkala had a Cherokee wife and two children (p. 42) who lived with him inside a large cave in Tanasee Bald atop which he had his farm (site 29). The petroglyphs on Judaculla Rock (literally Tsulkala Rock), about 4 miles east of Cullowhee, Jackson Co., North Carolina, are said to be the marks made by Tsulkala's feet when he leaped from the mountain down to the creek bank (see also sites 7, 54).

THE MYTHIC PLACES
"WHERE LEGENDS LIVE"
(Use map in back of book [p. 48] as a guide)

Explanation of "Mythic Places" Entries

Agisiyi . . . . Common rendering of name.

(Akihsi:yi) . . . . Phonetic rendering of name.

"The place of the female" . . . . Translation of the name.

(See #1 on Map) . . . . Reference to map in the back of the book (pg. 48)

On the Tuckasegee River where U.S. 19 crosses it about 2 miles east
of Bryson City, Swain Co., North Carolina. . . . . Location

Comments: Several supernatural "white people" (speaking in a magical
rather than a racial sense) were seen washing clothes in the river and . . . . Comments on the place containing history,
drying them on the bank at this spot. These beings apparently belonged   significance, and other helpful information.
to the family of the mythical Agehya Egwa *(Akehya-e:kwa,* "Big Female").

Agisiyi
(Akihsi:yi)
"The place of the female"
(See #1 on Map)

On the Tuckasegee River where U.S. 19 crosses it about 2 miles east of Bryson City, Swain Co., North Carolina.

Comments: Several supernatural "white people" (speaking in a magical rather than a racial sense) were seen washing clothes in the river and drying them on the bank at this spot. These beings apparently belonged to the family of the mythical Agehya Egwa *(Akehya-e:kwa,* "Big Female").

12

The Death of the Uktena
by Nancy-Lou Patterson

Agwediyi

(Ahkweti':yi)

"The place of the lizard monster"

(See #2 on Map)

A spot on the Tuckasegee River between the mouth of Dick's Creek and the upper end of the Cowee tunnel. It can best be seen from the junction of N.C. 107 and U.S. 19A & 441 on the N.W. side of Dillsboro, Jackson Co., North Carolina.

Comments: A dangerous water monster (presumably some sort of giant lizard) is supposed to live in the river here.

Ahalunuh-yi

(A:halunv':ʔi)

"Ambush Place"

(See #3 on Map)

Soco Gap, where U.S. 19 crosses the Haywood-Jackson county line, North Carolina.

Comments: A nest of giant yellowjackets located just east of the gap was destroyed by the Little People. This site is almost certainly identical with the *Ahlun'ui* (South Side Gap) reported by Kilpatrick and Kilpatrick, (1966).

Atsilawo-i

(Atsi:lawo:ʔi')

"Where fire comes down"
(See #4 on Map)

Rattlesnake Mountain, 2 miles N.E. of the town of Cherokee, Swain Co., North Carolina. A good view is from the road that runs in front of the Indian Hospital in Cherokee.

Comments: A sacred divining crystal, the Uluhsati, was seen to fly through the air as a ball of fire and land on this mountain. It had been hidden there by its owner and, after his death, it flew out each night to seek him. Could this be the same Uluhsati that "Groundhogs' Mother" brought back to the Cherokee from Gahuhdi?

Dadliyasdiha

(Ta:tli ʔyahstiha)

"He fell on his back"
(See #5 on Map)

On the Tuckasegee River at the bend upstream from Webster, Jackson Co., North Carolina. It can best be seen from the gravel road that runs along the bank of the river.

Comments: Two large Uktenas, entwined as if fighting, were once seen to lift part of their bodies out of a deep hole in the river and then fall back into the water.

The Hunter in the Dagwuh
by Nancy-Lou Patterson

15

Dagwuh-i

(Ta:ʔkwvʔi)
"Dagwuh place"
(See #6 on Map)

The French Broad River at Sandy Bottom, approximately 4 miles by winding dirt road west of Walnut, Madison Co., N.C. This site is on private property and not accessible to the public.

Comments: A monster fish lives here.

Datsuna-laskuh-i

(Tatsu:naʔlahskv':ʔi)
"Where the tracks are"
(See #7 on Map)

Shining Rock, Haywood Co., N.C. It can be reached by trail from the trailhead parking areas (approximately 4¼ miles one way); both of the parking areas are accessible from the Blue Ridge Parkway.

Comments: The name refers to a rock at the base of the mountain that has markings on it said to be footprints left by Tsulkala and his family when they were returning to their home on Tanasee Bald. We were not able to locate the rock or to determine if it still exists. Inside the mountain is a dwelling place of the Nuhnehi.

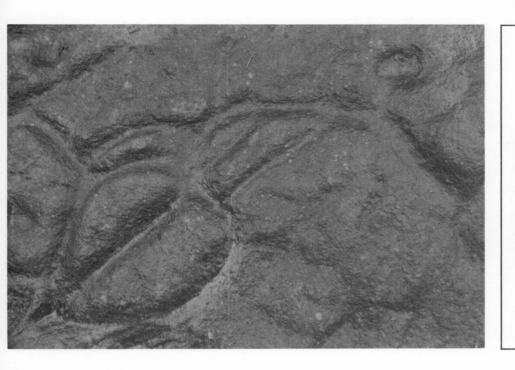

Datsuna-laskuh-i

(Tatsu:na ʔlahskv':ʔi)

"Where the tracks are"

(See #8 on Map)

Track Rock Gap, 4½ airline miles east of Blairsville, Union Co., Georgia. Take U.S. 76 approximately 6½ miles E.N.E. from its junction with U.S. 19 & 129 and turn south on the paved road marked with a Track Rock Gap Archeological Area sign.

Comments: The petroglyphs on the rocks here are generally similar to those found on Judaculla Rock and are said to be tracks left, when the newly created earth was still soft, by a hoard of animals fleeing through the Gap to escape some pursuing danger from the west.

Duniskwaluh-yi

(Tu:nihskwalv:yi)

"Place of the forked antlers"

(See #9 on Map)

Indian Gap, Swain Co., North Carolina-Sevier Co., Tennessee. It can be seen on the northern side of the road that runs from Newfound Gap to Clingman's Dome, 1¼ miles from its junction with U.S. 441.

Comments: On his search for the great Uktena, Oganunitsi encountered an unspecified monster reptile when he passed by this spot.

Gadegwohi
(Ka'ɂt'e:kwo'hi)
"A lot of land"
(See #10 on Map)

Fodderstack Mountain, approximately 1¼ miles S.E. of Highlands, Macon Co., North Carolina. It can be seen easily from Horse Cove Road (inquire locally).

Comments: This is one of four mountains beneath which the bears have a council house where they hold a dance before denning up for the winter.

Gadu-diyi
(Ka:tuɂti':yi)
"A place of bread" [i. e., a place for a town]
(See #11 on Map)

Stratton Bald, Graham Co., North Carolina. It can reached by trail (approximately 7 miles one way) from the Joyce Kilmer Memorial Forest parking lot.

Comments: Some people started to build a settlement here but were frightened off by a strange noise they thought was made by an Uktena.

Gahuhdi

(Kahv:ʔti)

"The finishing place"

(See #12 on Map)

Cohutta Mountains in Murray Co., Georgia. The site can best be seen at Fort Mountain State Park off U.S. 76, approximately 7 miles east of Chatsworth, Georgia.

Comments: This is the place where "Groundhogs' Mother" finally found and killed the great Uktena. The 855-foot-long rock wall that meanders across the southern face of the mountain does not fit the description of the circular trench within which "Groundhogs' Mother" took refuge, but some of the larger "gunpits" along the wall might qualify. Although the surviving version of the myth relates that the bones of the dead Uktena were consumed by birds along with its flesh, that does not sound altogether reasonable and one wonders if, in an earlier version, the wall might not have represented the serpent's skeleton. Certainly the serpentine wall does remind one somewhat of the Great Serpent Mound in Ohio. Another large mythical serpent, the Ustuhtli *(U:hstv'hthli),* also lives on this mountain range. It moved about not by crawling but like an inchworm on its flat, three-cornered feet. The Ustuhtli made its presence known by bleating like a fawn, a sound that struck fear in the hearts of all hunters who heard it in the woods. It was finally killed by a hunter who set a fire around the base of the mountain that spread upward to the summit. The two stories seem to be related, although in one instance a protective fire encircled the man and in the other a destructive fire encircled the serpent.

Gigohi

(Ki:ko'hi)

"Blood place"

(See #13 on Map)

Blood Mountain, 1 mile W.N.W. of Neel's Gap, Union-Lumpkin Cos., Georgia. This view is from the northern side of the mountain on U.S. 19 and 129.

Comments: A council house of the Nuhnehi lies beneath this mountain.

Gihli-dinehuh-i

(Ki:hliti:nehv':ʔi)

"Place of the dogs"

(See #14 on Map)

A deep pool in the Oconaluftee River behind the Pink Motel on U.S. 441 in the town of Cherokee, Swain Co., North Carolina.

Comments: Two "red dogs," which normally live underwater, were once seen playing on the bank here.

20

Kitu-hwa

(Kitu'hwa)

''The middle''

(See #15 on Map)

Approximately 3 miles N.E. of Bryson City, Swain Co., North Carolina, on U.S. 19. The mound lies in a cultivated field on the south side of the highway a short distance behind a converted airplane hanger.

Comments: The mound at this former village site is said to contain a perpetual fire. The extremely important settlement here gave its name to one of the Cherokee dialects and, on ocasion, to the tribe as a whole *(Ani:kitu'hwa,* ''People of Kitu-hwa''); Mooney referred to it as one of the ''seven mother towns.'' Unlike the Nikwasi Mound in Franklin, North Carolina, the Kitu-hwa Mound is not protected. If it continues to be subjected to cultivation, it will not be long before all that remains of what once was the principal ceremonial center of the Eastern Cherokee will be lost forever.

Kuwo-i

(Khuwo': ʔi)

''Mulberry Place

(See #16 on Map)

Clingman's Dome, Swain Co., North Carolina-Sevier Co., Tennessee. At the crest of the Great Smoky Mountains on U.S. 441 take the spur road to the southwest for approximately 6 miles. The Dome can be reached by trail (approximately ½ mile one way) from the parking lot.

Comments: This is one of four mountains beneath which the bears have a council house where they hold a dance before denning up for the winter.

Nikwasi

(Ni:kwahsi)

The name cannot be translated

(See #17 on Map)

Next to U.S. 441 (business route) in downtown Franklin, Macon Co., North Carolina.

Comments: The mound at this former village site is said to contain a perpetual fire. A council house of the Nuhnehi lies beneath the mound and on one occasion, when the resident Cherokee were hard pressed by enemy warriors, a band of invisible Nuhnehi came out of the mound with their magic weapons and helped repel the attackers.

Nugatsani

(Nu:ʔkatsaʔni)

The name cannot be translated

(See #18 on Map)

The ridge south of the Oconaluftee River in the town of Cherokee, Swain Co., North Carolina. It can best be seen from U.S. 19 & 441.

Comments: The ridge is a dwelling place of the Nuhnehi.

Nuhdayehli

(Nv:tayehli)
"Midday sun"
(See #19 on Map)

Nantahala Gorge in Swain and Macon Cos., North Carolina. The lower gorge is traversed by U.S. 19 south of Wesser, the upper gorge by the Beechertown road (N.C. 1400). A scenic overview of the lower gorge is visible on U.S. 129 between Topton and Robbinsville.

Comments: The name "Midday sun" refers to the fact that, at places, the Nantahala Gorge is so narrow and steepwalled that sunlight cannot reach the bottom of it until late morning. The gorge was a favorite haunt of "Spearfinger" and it also has a resident giant serpent, the Uwtsuhta *(Uhw:tsv':ta)*. Like its counterpart, the Ustuhtli, in the Cohutta Mountains of Georgia, the Uwtsuhta moves about like an inchworm, but apparently without benefit of feet or bleat. It is so enormous that it casts a shadow whenever it stretches from one rim of the gorge to the other (p. 38). There are no tales of its death.

Saligugi

(Sali:ku:ki)
"Turtle place"
(See #20 on Map)

A deep hole in the Oconaluftee River where it makes a sharp bend approximately ½ mile S.W. of Birdtown along U.S. 19, Swain Co., North Carolina.

Comments: A monster turtle lives here.

Sanigilagi
(Sa:ni:kila:ki)

"The place where they took it out"
(See #21 on Map)

Whiteside Mountain, Jackson Co., North Carolina. It can best be seen from the top of Bearpen Mountain in Highlands (inquire locally).

Comments: The name refers to the destruction by the Thunders of the western summit of the mountain, which formed the eastern end of Spearfinger's great rock bridge.

Sehwaduh-yi
(Sehwatv:yi)

"Hornet place"
(See #22 on Map)

Cheoah and Swim Balds, Graham-Swain Cos., North Carolina. The best view is from Stecoah Gap on the road from Stecoah to Robbinsville. Cheoah Bald can be reached via the Appalachian Trail from Stecoah Gap (8½ miles one way).

Comments: A fierce monster hornet nested on this ridge and sunned itself on the balds. Until it finally disappeared, it drove away everyone who came here.

Sohiyi

(Sohi':yi)

"Place of the hickory nut"

(See #23 on Map)

Chimney Rock (southern side of Hickorynut Gorge), Rutherford Co., North Carolina.

Comments: Legend has it that a Cherokee conjuror, in the guise of hummingbird, flew down through Hickorynut Gorge to recover the tobacco plant for his people. After having done so, he turned himself into a whirlwind and, crossing Hickorynut Gap, scoured the walls of the Gorge in revenge upon the Little People for the death of a previous tobacco seeker. Finding the bones of the young man in the streambed, he restored him to life and the two of them brought back huge quantities of tobacco to Cherokee country, where it has flourished ever since.

Tiyohaliyi

(Thiyoha ʔli':yi)

"Lizard place"

(See #24 on Map)

Joanna Bald, Graham-Cherokee Co., North Carolina. It can be reached by a gravel road running east from the Robbinsville-Andrews road.

Comments: A giant rough-scaled lizard was frequently seen sunning on the rocky slopes. The top of Joanna Bald today is covered by buildings, so in the interest of capturing the essence of the original setting we have taken a little artistic license and present here a photograph of another bald area on the same ridge a mile or so to the east along the Bartram Trail.

Tlanusiyi

(Tla:nuʔsiʹyi)

"Leech place"

(See #25 on Map)

Pool and ledge in the Valley River near its junction with the Hiwassee River at Murphy, Cherokee Co., North Carolina. It is located beneath the bridge at the foot of Tennessee Street.

Comments: A giant leech used to lie on the ledge above a deep hole in the river. When it would fall into the pool and wriggle about, the resulting wave would sweep anyone crossing the stream off the ledge and into the pool where the leech would consume them (p. 29). The town of Murphy, which was built on the site of a former Cherokee village, is still known as "Leech place" to the Cherokee people.

Tlanuwo-i

(Thlanu:woʹ:ʔi)

"Tlanuwa place"

(See #26 on Map)

A large bluff on the northern side of the Little Tennessee River just downstream and across from the mouth of Citico Creek, Blount Co., Tennessee. It can best be seen by looking westward from the boat landing that is adjacent to the point where U.S. 129 turns northward away from the river.

Comments: This is the bluff where the pair of Tlanuwas, discussed in the introduction, had their nest.

Tsisduyi

(Tsihstu:yi)

"Rabbit place"

(See #27 on Map)

Gregory Bald, Swain Co., N.C.-Blount Co., Tennessee. The site is accessible by trail from the Cades Cove trailhead (5 miles one way).

Comments: The rabbits have a council house beneath this mountain and it is here that their chief, the Great Rabbit, lives. This also is one of four mountains beneath which the bears have a council house where they hold a dance before denning up for the winter.

Tsudatsinasuh-i

Tsu:tatsi:nahsv':?i

"Over at the deep place"

(See #28 on Map)

A deep hole at the junction of Cochran Creek and the Cheoah River, Graham Co., North Carolina. It lies along U.S. 129 a short distance north of the Santeetlah Dam.

Comments: An eddy in the Cheoah River at this spot was said to be caused by an underwater buffalo (bison) that moved here from Yanso-i. With the damming of the river, the slowing of its flow, and the accumulation of silt, the eddy has disappeared.

Tsuneguh-yi
(Tsu:ne:kv':yi)
"The white places"
(See #29 on Map)

Tanasee Bald, Jackson-Transylvania Cos., North Carolina. It can best be reached by taking the trail south from the parking lot at the junction of the Blue Ridge Parkway and N.C. 215.

Comments: Tsulkala, the slant-eyed giant, lives in a cave inside this mountain and had his farm on the bald. Judaculla Rock, for which there apparently is no Cherokee name, is part of the same myth (see the Introduction) and is pictured below. It is one of only three mythic sites that have been protected and given an informational marker. Judaculla Rock is located near Caney Fork, approximately 4 miles east of Cullowhee, Jackson Co., North Carolina.

The Great Leech of Tlanusiyi
by Nancy-Lou Patterson

29

Tsuwatelda
(Tsuwa'hthelta)
"He hovers over it"
(See #30 on Map)

Pilot Mountain, Transylvania Co., North Carolina. Take U.S. 276 west for 5¼ miles from its junction with U.S. 64 at Brevard. Turn left on the Pisgah Forest National Fish Hatchery road and proceed 6¼ miles to Gloucester Gap. If the gate on the righthand road is open you can drive up onto the slope of Pilot Mountain; if the gate is locked, park at the gap and hike up the trail that leaves the road at that point.

Comments: The place name probably refers to the fact that it was thought Thunder, Kanati--along with his wife Selu and the Thunder boys, once lived at the very top of Pilot Mountain. This being the case, presumably the cave from which all game animals originally emerged opened somewhere on its slopes. A council house of the Nuhnehi lies beneath this mountain.

Tsuwa-uniyetsguh-i
(Tsu'wa-u:ni:ye:thsk:v'?i)
"Where the waterdogs laughed"
(See #31 on Map)

Tusquitee Bald, Macon-Clay Cos., North Carolina. It is visible from the Bob Allison Camping Area, which is reached by a gravel Forest Service road running north from the community of Tusquitee.

Comments: A hunter crossing over this mountain during the dry season spied two large salamanders walking along the trail on their hindlegs and joking about the drought. They had abandoned their drying pond and were on their way to the Nantahala River.

Udawoguhda
(U:tawo:ʔkv':ta)
"The mountain is bald"
(See #32 on Map)

Big Bald Mountain, Yancey Co., North Carolina-Unicoi Co., Tennessee. It can be reached by the Appalachian Trail from U.S. 23 at Sam's Gap (6 miles one way).

Comments: Atop Bald Mountain, Oganunitsi encountered a giant rough-scaled lizard during his search for the great Uktena. Mooney indicated only that Bald Mountain lies on the Tennessee-North Carolina line northeastward from Big Pigeon River. Several mountains in Madison and Yancey counties could fit this description; if the one pictured here is not the actual site in question, it is at least representative in appearance.

Udiguhi
(Uʔ:tiku'hi)
"Where the whirlpool is"
(See #33 on Map)

An eddy in the Tennessee River near the mouth of Suck Creek, Marion Co., Tennessee. Take Tennessee 27 west from Chattanooga to Suck Creek.

Comments: The eddy that was present in the river near the creek's mouth, before it was "drowned" beneath Nickajack Lake, marked the spot where the pot containing Lightning was thrown into the river (see the Introduction for more details).

Uguh-yi
(U:kv:ʔyi')
"The place behind the water"
(See #34 on Map)

Tallulah Falls, Rabun Co., Georgia. U.S. 23-441 crosses the dam that was built just above the falls.

Comments: A family of Thunder Beings used to live beneath the falls, which have since been reduced to a trickle by the construction of the dam. The gorge below remains an awesome sight.

Uktena-tsuganuhdasuh-i
(U:khthe:nv-tsu:kaʔnv:tʔahsv':ʔi)
"Where the Uktena became entangled"
(See #35 on Map)

On the Tuckasegee River, about 2 miles above Deep Creek, Bryson City, Swain Co., North Carolina. The site lies on the western side of the U.S. 19 bridge.

Comments: An Uktena that was heading upstream became stuck between some rocks in the river bottom. In struggling to free itself, the giant serpent pried up some large rocks and left deep scratches in others along the bank.

Uktena-udansinuhsduh-i

(U:khthe:nv-u:tansi:nv̓stv'ʔi)

"Where the Uktena just crawled"

(See #36 on Map)

On the Tuckasegee River, about 4 river miles above Bryson City, Swain Co., North Carolina. Any of a number of rocks east of the railroad bridge crossing would seem to fit Mooney's description.

Comments: An Uktena left depressions in the rocks in and along the river bed as it crawled upstream. These rocks are most easily seen during periods of low water.

Lightning and the Gambler, Uhtsayi
by Nancy-Lou Patterson

34

Ukteniyi

(U:khthe:ni':yi)

"Uktena place"
(See #37 on Map)

A deep hole in the Oconaluftee River in Cherokee, Swain Co, North Carolina. It is situated wher the river takes a sharp eastward bend just downstream from the bridge at the intersection of U.S. 441 and U.S. 19.

Comments: Several Uktenas have been seen in the river here.

Utlanuwa

(Uh:thla''?nu:wa)

"The Tlanuwa reaches over it"
(See #38 on Map)

The bluff at the foot of Market Street in Chattanooga, Hamilton Co., Tennessee. The best view is from the northern side of the river.

Comments: The bluff presumably was once a Tlanuwa nesting site.

Waginsi
(Wakinsi)
"This is where I have been placed"
(See #39 on Map)

An eddy in the Tennessee River at its junction with the Little Tennessee River opposite Lenior City, Loudon Co., Tennessee.

Comments: There used to be a large eddy, now submerged, at the mouth of the Little Tennessee where a large serpent lived. To see it was an omen of evil. Tellico Dam is just visible in the background; the lake it formed certainly was a manifestation of bad luck for the Cherokee, since it flooded the site of Echota, the Overhill "White Town" and capital of the Cherokee Nation just before the Removal of 1838. The lower picture shows the site of Echota (across the Little Tennessee) as it appeared in 1969 before Tellico Lake was formed.

Walosiyi

(Walo:ʔsi':yi)

''Frog place''
(See #40 on Map)

A gap on the ridge between Mount LeConte and Balsam Point, Sevier Co., Tennessee.

Comments: According to Mooney, this name applies to a gap somewhere along the ridge between Mt. LeConte and Bullhead Mountain. A comparison of maps made early in this century with more recent ones reveals that in Mooney's time the latter name was applied to the peak now known as Balsam Point. Oganunitsi found a giant frog squatting in the gap when he passed through this area during his search for the giant Uktena.

Yonä-dinehuh-i

(Yo:na-ti:nehv':ʔi)

''Where the bears live over there''
(See #41 on Map)

A deep hole in the Oconaluftee River, about 1 mile above its junction with the Tuckasegee River, Swain Co., North Carolina. Take the gravel road that turns off to the east from the Whittier highway and runs along the south bank of the Oconaluftee. Park just beyond a hairpin bend in the road and take a short, but steep, trail down to the river.

Comments: A family of ''water bears'' live at the bottom of the deep hole.

Uwtsuhta, the Inchworm Serpent
by Nancy-Lou Patterson

Yuhwi-tsulenuh-i

(Yv:wi-tsu:lehnv:ʔi)

"The place where the person stood"

(See #42 on Map)

Standing Indian, Macon-Clay Cos., North Carolina. It can be reached by the Appalachian Trail from Deep Gap (about 3 miles one way).

Comments: A mysterious being was said to have been seen standing on the mountaintop.

Adagahi

(A:takahi')

"Gall place"

On the northern boundary of Swain Co., North Carolina, between the headwaters of Bradley's Fork and Eagle Creek.

Comments: *A:takahi'* is the invisible medicine lake where wounded animals go to be healed. Its purple waters can only be seen at dawn by one who has fasted and kept a night-long vigil.

Dagwuh-i

(Ta:ʔkwvʔi)

"Dagwuh place"
(See #44 on Map)

The Little Tennessee River at the mouth of Toquo Creek, Blount Co., Tennessee.

Comments: This is where the Cherokee version of the Jonah or Hiawatha legend took place. A giant fish swallowed a warrior (p. 15) who finally managed to cut his way out of the fish's gut with a mussel shell. The site is one of those "drowned" by Tellico Lake.

Dotsiyi

(Totsi:yi)

"Dotsi place"
(See #45 on Map)

On the Little Tennessee River just upstream from the mouth of Eagle Creek, Graham-Swain Cos., North Carolina.

Comments: Mooney noted that the Dotsi is a traditional water monster. One was supposed to live in a deep hole here, but the site now lies beneath Fontana Lake.

Dustayohluh-i

(Tuhstayohlv':ʔi)

"Where he shot"
(See #46 on Map)

On the Hiwassee River at the mouth of Shooting Creek, Clay Co., North Carolina.

Comments: The people who lived in the village near here were taken to live underwater with the Nuhnehi and on warm summer days they occasionally could still be heard talking beneath the water. The site has been submerged beneath Hiwassee Reservoir.

Gusti

(Kuhsti')

"The place where something is in the water"
(See #47 on Map)

A place in the Tennessee River near Kingston, Roane, Co., Tennessee.

Comments: There is a council house underwater here, and sometimes the sound of drums can still be heard. The location is too vague to be easily located.

Nuhyodluguh-i

(Nvʔyoʹtluhkvʹ:ʔi)

"Where the tree is on the rock"
(See #48 on Map)

Tree Rock, on the western side of the Hiwassee River, approximately 4 miles upstream from Hayesville, Clay Co., North Carolina.

Comments: This rock formed the western base of Spearfinger's great rock bridge, which was destroyed by lightning. It could not be located.

Setsi

(Sehtsi')

The name cannot be translated

A large mound on the southern side of the Valley River, approximately 2 miles W.S.W. of Andrews, Cherokee Co., North Carolina.

Comments: The mound was said to be part of the *Anihskayvʹ:yi* (Men town") council house that fell off while the Nuhnehi were moving it through the air to the high ridge west of the lower Nantahala Gorge. The mound has completely disappeared due to the effects of years of cultivation, but pottery fragments can still be found occasionally to mark its former location.

Tlanuwo-atsiyeluhsuh-i

(Thlanu:woʹ:a:tsi:ye:lvʔsvʹ:ʔi)

"Where the Tlanuwa cut it up"
(See #50 on Map)

On the Little Tennessee River opposite the mouth of Citico Creek, Blount Co., Tennessee.

Comments: A rock whose surface bears a series of long trenchlike depressions made by the pieces of an Uktena that was torn apart by a pair of Tlanuwas, was situated on the northern side of the river just below Tallassee Ford. It now lies beneath the surface of Tellico Lake.

Tsulkala, the Slant-Eyed Giant
by Nancy-Lou Patterson

Tsgaguh-yi

(Thska ʔkv:yi)

"Yellowjacket place"

A cave on the eastern side of the valley where Franklin, Macon Co., North Carolina, is located.

Comments: A giant yellowjacket (*U:ʔlohka*), which had been carrying off children from a Cherokee village on the Nantahala River, was trailed to its lair in the cave and killed by smoke. The cave has not been located.

Tsudayeluh-i

(Tsu:taye:ʔlv':ʔi)

"Where it was left alone"

Lone Peak, near Cheoah Bald, Graham Co., North Carolina.

Comments: The council house from *Anihskayv':yi* ("Men town") was carried off through the air by the Nuhnehi and deposited on the top of this mountain. Lone Peak does not appear on the most detailed topographic maps, and it is not known locally.

Tsukiluhnuh-i

(Tsuhkhilv:ʔnv':ʔi)

"The elevated place where he once stood"

Two small balds on the side of the mountain at the head of Little Snowbird Creek, Graham Co., North Carolina.

Comments: A mysterious giant with a blazing head (some think it may have been the Sun) was seen once to fly through the air, land on this mountain, and stand for some time surveying the view before flying off again. The description of the mountain is somewhat vague, but it might be McDaniel Bald.

Tsulasinuh-i

(Tsu:la:ʔsihnv':ʔi)

"Where he stepped"
(See #54 on Map)

On the northern side of the Tuckasegee River, approximately 1 mile upstream from Deep Creek, Swain Co., North Carolina.

Comments: A rock, whose surface was said to bear the footprints of Tsulkala and a deer, used to be situated at this spot but had already been blasted out for the railroad line in Mooney's time.

Utluhtuyi

(Uthlvhtu:yi')

"Spearfinger place"

(See #55 on Map)

On the Little Tennessee River almost opposite the mouth of Citico Creek, Blount Co., Tennessee (however, Mooney also said it was on the other side of the river from Tlanuwo-i).

Comments: This was one of Spearfinger's favorite lurking places.

Uyahyehi

(U:yaʔhyehi)

"The mountain that holds something"

This mountain in the Great Smokies cannot be identified.

Comments: This is one of four mountains beneath which the bears have a council house where they hold a dance before denning up for the winter. Its location is unknown.

Yanso-i

(Ya:nso':ʔi)

"Buffalo place"

(See #57 on Map)

The junction of West Buffalo Creek and the Cheoah River, Graham Co., North Carolina.

Comments: An underwater buffalo (bison) once lived here before migrating to Tsudatsinasuh-i. The site is now covered by Santeetlah Lake.

Yona-unadawosidiyi

(Yo:na-u:natawo:ʔsti':yi)

"Where the bears take a bath"

(See #58 on Map)

The extreme headwaters of the Raven Fork of the Oconaluftee River, Swain Co., North Carolina.

Comments: This pond of cold purple water (which had nearly dried up in Mooney's time and by now has presumably disappeared) was a favorite bear wallow and was thought by some to possess the same healing properties as the better-known Adagahi.

LITERATURE CITED

Bushyhead, Robert, and Bill Cook
No Date. *Cherokee Lessons.* Unpublished manuscript, Museum of the Cherokee Indian, Cherokee, North Carolina.

Campbell, Joseph
1973. *Myths To Live by.* Bantam Books, New York, xiv + 288 pp.

Fogelson, Raymond
1982. Cherokee Little People Reconsidered. *Journal of Cherokee Studies* 7(2):92-98.

Howard, James H.
1976. The Southeastern Ceremonial Complex and Its Interpretation. *Memoir of the Missouri Archeological Society* (6): 1-169.

Hudson, Charles
1976. *The Southeastern Indians.* University of Tennessee Press, Knoxville, xviii + 573 pp.

Hudson, Charles
1978. Uktena: A Cherokee Anomalous Monter. *Journal of Cherokee Studies* 3(2):62-75.

Kilpatrick, Jack F., and Anna G. Kilpatrick
1966. Anthropological Papers, No. 80. Eastern Cherokee Folktales: Reconstructed from the Field Notes of Frans M. Olbrechts. *Bulletin of the Bureau of American Ethnology* (196): 379-447.

Mooney, James
1900. Myths of the Cherokee. *19th Annual Report of the Bureau of American Ethnology:* 3-576.

Witthoft, John
1946. Bird Lore of the Eastern Cherokee. *Journal of the Washington Academy of Science* 36:372-384.

INDEX OF MYTHICAL BEINGS

The number following each name refers to the page in the text where the being is most fully described. Although the Uluhsati would not ordinarily be considered a being, at times it does seem to have a life of its own (see page 14) and is included here for convenience sake.

The Tlanuwas and the Uktena
by Nancy-Lou Patterson

47

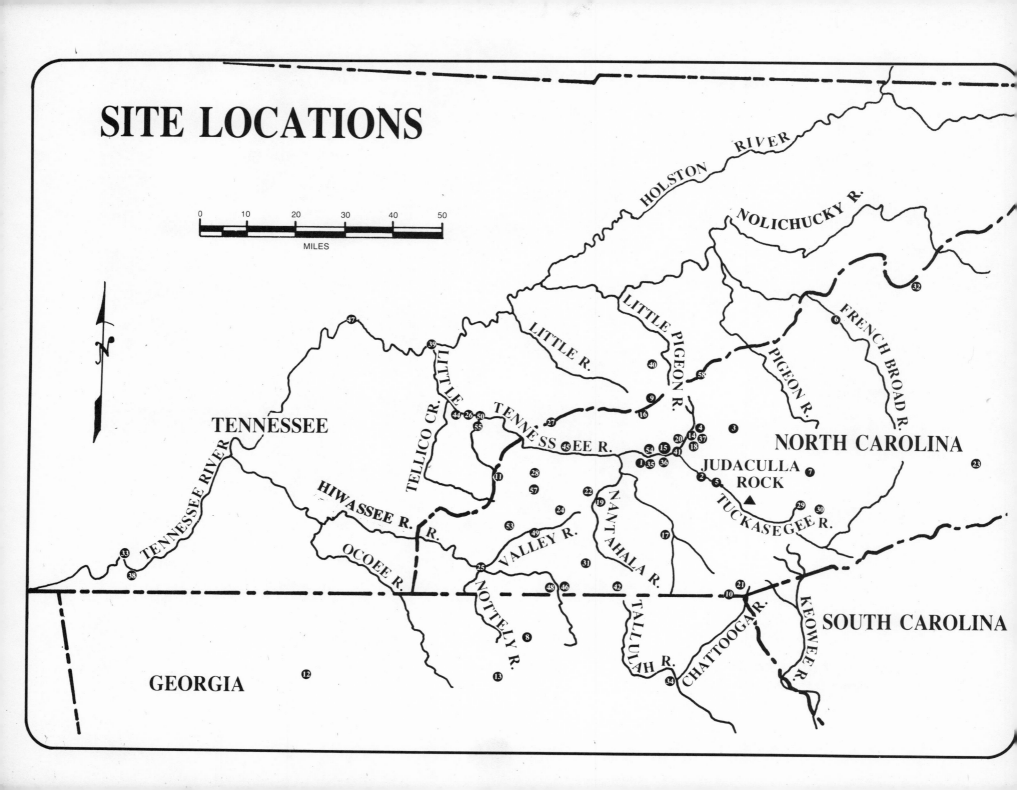

SITE LOCATIONS

TENNESSEE

NORTH CAROLINA

SOUTH CAROLINA

GEORGIA

JUDACULLA ROCK

HOLSTON RIVER

NOLICHUCKY R.

FRENCH BROAD R.

LITTLE PIGEON R.

LITTLE R.

PIGEON R.

LITTLE

TELLICO CR.

TENNESSEE R.

TENNESSEE RIVER

HIWASSEE R. R.

OCOEE R.

NOTTELY R.

VALLEY R.

NANTAHALA R.

TALLULAH R.

TUCKASEGEE R.

CHATTOOGA R.

KEOWEE R.

MILES